RAPING THE GOLD

by Lucy Gannon

CHAPPELL PLAYS

LONDON

A member of the Chappell and Intersong Music Group

First published 1988 by
Chappell Plays Ltd
129 Park Street, London W1Y 3FA

© Copyright Lucy Gannon, 1988

ISBN 0 85676 141 9

Typeset and printed by Commercial Colour Press, London E7.
Cover design by Helen Lannaghan.

RAPING THE GOLD was first presented at the Bush Theatre, London on 28th March 1988, with the following cast:

Stuart	Paul Copley
Zip	Charlie Creed-Miles
Leon	Paterson Joseph
Gabby	Trevor Peacock
Sally	Sophie Thursfield
Joe	Arthur Whybrow
James	Henry Woolley

Directed by Debbie Shewell
Designed by Paul Brown
Lighting by Ben Ormerod

The play takes place over four weeks in a small Derbyshire town. The time is the present.

ARCHERY NOTES

The play was written with a large theatre in mind, but was given its first production at the Bush Theatre, a very small theatre indeed. Originally I had envisaged the archery practice taking place above the rest of the action, the target being some distance away, as it is in real life. However, the designer Paul Brown, and the director, Debbie Shewell worked a small miracle both with the set and with the play, and I was very happy indeed with the production.

As I originally intended, the bow that Gabby uses in the first act is fitted with a device used by keen archers for indoor practice in inclement weather. It is a hollow tube attached to the centre of the riser, into which a rod, or 'arrow' is shot. Because most archers have stabiliser rods attached to their bows, this device does not look unsightly and we had a single, central stabiliser on Stuart's bow, so that the two looked similar. Gabby, Stuart and Sally all have composite bows.

Gabby's bow should be graceful and well cared for, whereas Stuart's can be shabby and a bit clumsy. The boys have fibre glass practice bows, and shabby club arrows.

In the Bush production the boys and Stuart never actually used arrows, but went through all the actions of archery practice holding the bows. In the same way, the target was unseen.

Gabby should have the poise of a good archer, the concentration and lack of self-consciousness of a fanatic, whereas Stuart is not, and never will be, a good archer.

Photograph by Nobby Clark from the Bush Theatre production of Raping the Gold

ACT ONE

Scene One

An archery field. While the stage is in darkness, we become aware of a vibration of sound, a pulse. The vibration grows into a clearly heard steady single beat. As it grows louder we hear the lub-dub of a heart beat, gradually increasing in speed as well as in volume. A light reveals a modern archer, GABBY, with his bow poised and an arrow ready for flight but not yet pulled back. The heart beat continues. He pulls back on the string, sights carefully, and then releases. GABBY slowly lowers his bow. He is totally absorbed by the sight of the arrow. Tensed with suppressed triumph, he slowly raises his bow towards the arrow as if offering the one to the other. The bow is balanced on the upturned palm of his hand. He bows his head and stands still for a long moment. He is in the centre of some ritual, awed by the emotion of the moment.

Very slowly he raises his arms and lifts the bow higher. His awe turns to exhileration, but is still controlled. The bow is above his head now, and he turns around slowly, a full 360 degrees as if showing the bow to the world. Gradually he speeds up the little steps with which he revolves, spinning around again and again, even faster, as if in a tribal dance of victory. He throws his head back and laughs. He brandishes the bow, thrusting it skywards, in the closed fist gesture of a football fanatic when a goal has been scored. He opens his mouth for what we know will be a shout, a deafening yell of triumph. The shout is never born. Offstage comes the sound of a car door slamming, followed by an oath and another attempt to slam the door. GABBY stands stock still, bow still raised, looking toward the sound, his mouth still open. STUART enters, hurrying towards him. He carries an archery case in one hand, a Thermos flask in the other, and a clipboard is under one arm. GABBY closes his mouth and stares at STUART. As STUART nears the stage, he drops the clip board, and noisily puts down the archery case. He unscrews the top of the flask. He doesn't look at GABBY.

STUART   If I've broken this she'll give me hell.

                (GABBY *slowly lowers his arms.* STUART *peers into the flask, shaking it slightly.*)

STUART   Thank God. (*Smiling up at* GABBY *ingenuously.*) Dropped it in the road, getting out of the car.

                STUART *opens his case to reveal several rows of shining arrows in the lid. As* STUART *talks* GABBY *turns away.*

STUART   (*assembling his bow*) I look forward to this all flaming day, you know. The little sods can do their worst from nine to four, so long as there's a chance to loose a few arrows at the end of it. Lost one last week, in the long grass over there.

(*He indicates but* GABBY *doesn't look*)

If you find it...Four quid a time these arrows are, not as good as yours of course...still...

(*When the bow is assembled he puts it down and looks around hopefully.*) So, the only ones here, then, are we?

STUART   I told them, I said, 'Be a bit early.' I said. I don't see a bit of extra practice doing them two youngsters any harm, do you? I told them a few minutes extra wouldn't kill them. But there you are...Try telling them...Flaming kids.

(*He moves towards* GABBY, *who immediately moves away.* STUART *follows him, smiling.* GABBY *puts his bow down so that it rests on its stand, as* STUART *watches.*)

STUART   Finished shooting?

(GABBY *stares at him.*)

STUART   Did I stop you? Were you shooting? (GABBY *shrugs.*) I didn't realise. I didn't mean to stop your practice. You should have said.

GABBY   It's all right, Stuart, I'm used to it.

(STUART *colours and turns away.* GABBY *takes a boiled sweet from his pocket and unwraps it deliberately, popping it into his mouth with a little flourish. He looks at* STUART *and holds a sweet out to him.* STUART *starts to shake his head, but then abruptly takes it.*)

STUART   Thanks. Save it for later, I think. I see that you've been getting some good scores. Club champion again this year, eh? (*Pause.*) I reckon you will be...Three years running that'll be...good show. (GABBY *merely looks down on his bow, smiling slightly.*)

STUART (*growing even more jerky, more wordy*) Sounds very Battle of Britain-ey, that, doesn't it? 'Good show'! (*He laughs, disclaiming the words.*) Brought up on the Rover and The Hotspur, so there you are! And the Eagle. Dan Dare. Those green men. Well, creatures.

(GABBY *crouches down and lightly caresses his bow.* STUART *paces around.*)

STUART Silent river, evening air, the buzz of distant insects, the target...Now, you can make it to the meeting?

GABBY Yes.

STUART Only, Gerry can't make it and we really could have done with him.

GABBY I'll be there.

STUART I can't put it off.

GABBY So you said.

STUART You'll see why.

GABBY (*sighing*) For God's sake, I'll be there. (*Pause.*) Are you shooting tonight?

STUART Probably. Later. You know.

GABBY Then bloody shoot. (*Pause.*) I won't watch. Promise. (STUART *winces as if he's been slapped.* GABBY *puts a hand out awkwardly and touches* STUART'S *shoulder.*)

GABBY Shoot if you want to.

(STUART *shakes his head.*)

JOE (*entering*) Ho! Archers!

(GABBY *raises a hand in a slow and courtly greeting.*)

STUART Joe! It's good to see you! My, it is good to see you. Here, let me give you a hand. (*He grabs an elbow.* JOE *testily slaps his hand away.*)

| JOE | Give over, will you. I'm old, not bloody daft. Ay up, then Gabriel. |
| GABBY | Joe. |

(They smile at each other. There is a sudden gentleness in GABBY. STUART mutters loudly to GABBY, from the side of his mouth.)

STUART	Marvellous how he keeps going, isn't it? Never misses Friday practice, come hell or high water.
JOE	And I'm not deaf, neither.
STUART	Of course not.
JOE	Hell or high water. Ay up, the day's coming when this club'll be two men and a Jack Russell. Is there no practice, then?
STUART	*(looking at his clip board)* There you are — Zip and young James. Zip Porter and James Anthony, junior practice, six o'clock, Friday, 9th September. So much for our junior champion and his ever faithful lackey.

(Towards the end of this GABBY has walked away and now sits in a cross-legged position, with his eyes closed. JOE takes his pipe out and fiddles with it.)

| STUART | *(with barely restrained bitterness)* He fortifies himself with his closed eyes, and we respect the high, deep walls of his fort. If he had put up the practice items they'd be here now, shooting, eagerly. They see his closed eyes, his smile and his sodding serenity and they fall down in submission. They sharpen their wicked little teeth for me. |

(ZIP, a fourteen year old in black denim arrives with a racing bike. Behind him labours fresh faced, slightly overweight JAMES, also fourteen. ZIP is yodelling Tarzan-like. He throws the bike down.)

| JAMES | *(shouting)* Hey! You twit, Zip! |

(JAMES picks the bike up and examines it for scratches.)

| ZIP | What? |

JAMES	Thanks. You could have buckled something.
STUART	I'll buckle something in a minute. What time do you call this?
JAMES	Are we late, then?
STUART	Oh, not to worry, lads. I like coming down here and giving up my evening just so that you two can come bowling in at whatever time you like. I like standing around like a wet Sunday.
ZIP	There you are. Told you he wouldn't mind.
STUART	Discipline! A little word we seem to have forgotten around here of late.
JAMES	My mum gave us tea.
STUART	Lucky you.
JAMES	We had to finish it.
STUART	Go and get your gear from the hut.
	(JAMES *leads the way.* ZIP *is about to argue.*)
STUART	I said —
ZIP	Where's Gerry?
STUART	Gerry? Gerry is on holiday. I'm coaching you this week.
ZIP	Only he teaches different from you — him not being a teacher.
STUART	Go and get your gear from the hut.
JAMES	(*exiting*) Come on, Zip.
	(ZIP *shrugs and follows. Stuart turns his attention to his clipboard.* SALLY *enters. She drops her case noisily,* GABBY *jumps but doesn't open his eyes.*)
SALLY	(*unnecessarily loud*) Hello Dad.
	(GABBY *opens his eyes.*)
GABBY	Ah. Sally. Are you all right?
SALLY	You weren't at home.

GABBY	No. I'm sorry, love.
SALLY	There wasn't any tea done.
GABBY	No.
SALLY	You promised. It was your turn.
GABBY	I'm sorry. I know —
SALLY	That's eighteen meals you owe me. And I bet there's nothing in for supper.
GABBY	I thought we could get chips.
SALLY	Chips! Again? It's not fair, Dad.
GABBY	Man does not live by —
SALLY	No. And he doesn't live by that thing either (*Indicating the bow.*)
GABBY	Time just sped past, love.
SALLY	How long have you been down here? (GABBY *looks at her.*)
SALLY	You've been here all day, haven't you? God, I give up.

(*She flounces off with her case and drops down nearby. She opens her case and takes out her quiver, putting it on sullenly.* GABBY *watches her for a moment and then closes his eyes again. As she does up her belt, etc.,* ZIP *and* JAMES *run back on stage with a fibre glass bow and a handful of arrows each. They slam to attention behind* STUART *with exaggerated military actions.*)

STUART	Oh yes. Very comical. Come on.

(*During the following dialogue* STUART *positions the boys and they prepare for shooting, with a degree of tomfoolery. The lighting on the stage dims and two spotlights pick out* JOE *and* SALLY. JOE *is watching her, puffing on his pipe. She has the centre of the bow in her hands.*)

SALLY	The riser. Rising from the box.

(SALLY *gets a real pleasure from the sound of words and she now looks over at* STUART *and mimics his voice.*)

Are you kids taking the rise out of me? Are you? Are you? (*She lifts out a limb from the case.*) A limb.

(*At one end of the limb is a screw and nut which she quickly takes apart.*)

SALLY   A Screw. I am screwing.

(*She mimics* GABBY'S *voice as she screws the limb to the riser.*)

'Don't call it screwing, Sally, not you. It's not to be spoken of like that, not by you. What would your mother have said?'

(*She looks over to* GABBY *and speaks normally but with great bitterness.*)

My mother would have said 'Fucking'. Nothing if not honest, my mother. Not totally honest, though, because she took out the nasty common 'U' and put in a nice refined 'A', so that it became altogether better, 'facking'. A part of the tennis-playing-theatre-going-gite-ing-in-France-facking-in-style set, my mother was. She would have said 'Facking' and then she would have laughed. Making it all all right. (*The bitterness goes and she continues to assemble her bow.*) When he puts his bow together he closes his eyes. He looks down at his case and a sort of daze comes over him. He's like a child unwrapping a present, all a rush at first and then going into a time warp, slowing down for that last uncovering, closing his eyes for those last few seconds, so that when the lid is open, it's all new and bright and startling. A contrast with the inside of his own eyelids. Anything looks good compared with that.

(*She looks around and adopts her mother's voice.*)

'Anything except facking Milsham.'

(*normally again*) I always know when he's coming
down here. Whatever he's doing, the crossword,
or the garden or the washing up, he speeds up.
Gets jerky. Like one of those old films. And he's
so busy hiding that excitement that he's deaf to
anything I say, and then I know that he's
thinking about this. And he marches along neat
pavements, stiff, up right, up tight, private and
locked in. Greedy. Greedy. I hate him when
he's like that. Then he opens the hut and brings
out a chair and puts his case on it, and he's like
a magician in the high spot of his show. I keep
expecting a roll of drums. That's when he closes
his eyes. It's only for a moment but I see it.
And the lid is laid back, and all his arrows are
laid out, lined up on the scarlet felt, red, black,
red, black, red, black. Dramatic. And he opens
his eyes and a great surge of pleasure runs
through his body and over his face. I have to
look away.

(*She stands to string the bow.*)

And he strokes that bow like his eyes used to
stroke my mother. Not his hands, of course, just
his eyes. But the bow lets him. And when he
strings it...when he strings it...he groans. Low
and deep.

(*She looks down at it.*) If he smoked he'd have a
fag afterwards.

(Zip *and* James *are talking together while* Stuart
shoots.)

James	What's your score?
Zip	Eighty seven.
James	Eighty seven! I've only got sixty one. Swap bows.
Zip	Get stuffed. You want to get what's on this side of the shooting line right before you start counting scores.

JAMES	All right. All right.
ZIP	I seen baboons with smaller bums than yours.
JAMES	I don't stick my bum out.
ZIP	And you got arms like a dog's back legs.
JAMES	I don't bend my wrists...
ZIP	You could get a YOP job as a contortionist, you could.
JAMES	I'm going to be a pilot. The Red Baron. Rat a tat tat.
ZIP	Sod off. Them lot lost. Firefox! (*He makes a swooshing sound.*)
JAMES	Firefox isn't real.
ZIP	So?
JAMES	The Red Baron is.
ZIP	He's dead, you prat. You bin talkin' to your dad again? You don't want to talk to your dad.
	Nearly as bad as him (*Indicating* STUART.)
	(JAMES *shrugs and looks over at* GABBY.)
JAMES	Do you think he's all right?
ZIP	Him? No, of course he isn't. Great, in't it? If we do really well we could end up like him...or him.
	(*The boys look from one man to the other as if watching tennis.*)
SALLY	(*still looking at her bow sadly*) It doesn't do a thing for me.
	(*The light fades on the boys who continue to fool around while* STUART *shoots.* GABBY *begins to hum on one resonant note, absorbed in his meditations.* SALLY *looks over to him.*)
JOE	Time was we had a score of young lads and lasses on the shooting line. Now we're lucky if we get half a dozen on 'em on a Sunday

afternoon. And Friday practice...well, they
want to be at the telly. A score of them we had.
(*Indicating* GABBY *and* STUART.) Him and him,
but a few years between them, of course. I gave
Gabby his first bow, a wooden hunting bow, it
was. And he loved that bow. When Eve died
and we went up there to pay our respects, there
it was, still. Up on the wall over the stair well in
that great big house, polished like bronze, new
string, new bindings, balanced on a mahogany
stand, for all the world to see. He's a good lad,
Gabby is. All those years he'd kept it, polished
it, oiled it, treasured it, must have. All those
years, top gaffer at the chain works, big cars,
long necked missus, jetting hither and yon, till it
all went bad on them, and still he kept that bow.
I daresay he has it still, even now he's not in
that grand house on the hill. I daresay he has. A
good lad.

(Zip *and* JAMES *break into a fight.* STUART *whirls
around to the two boys, lividly. As he shouts everyone
stops and looks at him, including* GABBY.)

STUART   Right! Right! You've got ten seconds to present
yourself for the next round, and if you aren't
ready there'll be club fines to pay and no entry
in the regional shoot next month!

(STUART *suddenly becomes aware of all the staring eyes.
Only* JOE *sees his embarrassment and looks away. It is
a long moment and* STUART *blusters.*)

STUART   Well, It *is* meant to be a club practice, not
bloody playtime. (*Pause.*) If discipline is to mean
anything. Anything at all.

(*Everyone gradually turns from him again and the boys
slowly pick up their bows and an arrow each to return
to the practice.* SALLY *has her bow extended and she is
looking through the sight at the audience. As she talks
she revolves slowly. Looking at individuals as she does
so. Lining them up in her sights.* JOE *is listening to
her.* GABBY *starts his humming again.*)

SALLY

I used to think that the High Street was like a mountain, so steep. Then we moved down south for a couple of years and when we came back...it had shrunk. Decayed and stooped, like a little old lady. Poor little old Milsham...That's how I thought of her — like a little old lady.

JOE

Milsham isn't what it was, but it was never that. It was never a lady. Leave being a lady to bloody Nottingham. Now *there's* a lady. All she was ever good for was lace. Menfolk living off of the backs of little lasses. And now it's all insurance offices and shops and bloody theatres. Menfolk still living off of the backs of wenches. Nottingham's a lady. Not Milsham.

SALLY

What's Derby?

JOE

Derby? Ah, Derby's another bloody thing entirely. Derby's a brat Derby is. But by Gad, she'll be a brat forever. They'll not down Derby.

SALLY

And Milsham?

JOE

(*with immense sadness*) And Milsham's a bloody liar.

(*they stare at each other in a moment of truth.*)

JAMES

(*yelling at* ZIP) You're a bloody liar! You're a bloody liar!

SALLY

(*lifting her bow again and looking through the sights, angling it higher*) And I spy at the top of the hill, the old china works. China moor they call it. Anywhere else it'd be a field, but up there it's a moor, a black wasteland, bordered by a vacant factory. Black chimneys giving the one up to every factory girl who ever dreamed of better.

ZIP

(*turning away from the archery and jerking one finger up in the air viciously*) Up yours! Up yours! Up yours!

SALLY	Not worth two up, Milsham isn't.
JOE	She bloody is. I'd give her two up any day, lying bitch that she is.
SALLY	I thought you'd have loved Milsham.
JOE	I do love her. The old bitch. Once she was full of young lasses like yourself. Lasses that spent long summer evenings playing rounders on the rec., queueing up outside the picture houses, putting on plays in the youth hall, saying to each other 'What'll you be?' By gad, that's a fine question, that is. 'What will you be when you leave school?' By Golly, that's a good question, that is. The old bitch.
SALLY	I used to want to be an air hostess.
JOE	(*laughing*) And I remember asking you one day, one day when your dad brought you down here and you sat over there with your dollies, 'Ay up, then, Sally, what do you want to be when you grow up?'
SALLY	I know.
JOE	Remember what you said?
SALLY	It was a long time ago.
JOE	You told me...

(*Everyone except* GABBY *stops to listen.*)

You told me, all six years of you, going on forty, 'I shall be the first lady astronaut...or a chip shop lady.'

(SALLY *slowly puts her bow down, and begins to tidy her case.*)

ZIP	(*to* JAMES) Funny, eh?
JAMES	Daft.
ZIP	My mam's a chip shop lady.

(*They glare at each other, and start to scuffle again.*)

STUART	Right, you two. Not a great practice tonight, was it? 'Could do better' is the phrase I'm searching for, I think.
ZIP	We did our best.
STUART	Oh, hardly.
JAMES	It was an off day.
STUART	We can't pick our days. No good saying at the Olympics, 'Sorry. Off day.' Is it? Going the wrong way on the handicap tables, as far as I can see, aren't we?
ZIP	Is our coach back next week?
STUART	I know the bows don't help.
	(*as* ZIP *slouches off*) Oy! Where do you think you're going? Zip!
	(JAMES *makes as if to follow* ZIP *but* STUART *grabs his arm.*)
	Hang on!
JAMES	I have to go. (*He slowly follows* ZIP.)
STUART	James!
	James! Zip!
	(JAMES *turns around to walk backwards, watching* STUART. ZIP *stops and waits for him to catch up.*)
STUART	Christ!
ZIP	And you needn't start on *him*.
	(STUART *turns back helplessly. He looks over to* GABBY *and is relieved to see that he still has his eyes closed. He tries to regain authority.*)
STUART	Now then, Sally.
SALLY	What?
STUART	You shooting?
SALLY	I'm not a junior.

STUART	I know that.
SALLY	I don't need a coaching session.
STUART	No. Of course not.

(She gets up and walks over.)

Just a couple of pointers, perhaps.

(She stops.)

Iron out any little faults that may be developing. I learnt a lot at that coaching course.

(SALLY turns back and walks away.)

Sally...

SALLY	I'm not shooting tonight. *(Taking pity on him.)* I wasn't really intending to shoot tonight. I just wanted to check my equipment. Honest.
JOE	The light's going, lad, best leave it.

(STUART and SALLY both unstring their bows and start to dismantle them. JOE gets up and walks slowly off. GABBY opens his eyes and waves once, then gets to his feet.)

GABBY	No bloody idea at all. A good night's work, eh Stuart? You might as well set fire to the bloody hut while you're at it.

(SALLY listens to them as she puts her bow away.)

STUART	There were sixty-seven school leavers in the town last year. Sixty-seven less for the school bus into Asby. Sixty-seven more for the dole. *(GABBY looks at him.)* I care about them. I can't help it. It's the way I am.
GABBY	I find it amusing when people tell me what *sort* of people they are. They are usually...very usual. Not requiring any explanation at all.
STUART	You couldn't care less, could you?
GABBY	We had a neighbour like you, once. She used to come in and drink tea with my mother.

(*Mimicing a foolish falsetto.*) 'I can't stand injustice, *I* can't.' (*Normally.*) Everyone else loves it, of course. (*Mimic.*) 'I hate it when people bite the heads off Yorkshire Terriers. I'm funny like that.' (*Pause.*) You're not the only one, Stuart. What do you want me to do? Slash an artery? Jump off a factory stack? What are you looking for?

STUART   Just remember to come to the meeting.

GABBY   For Christ's sweet sake. How many more times? What the hell has that to do with the school leavers anyway?

STUART   I can't tell you.

GABBY   Give me strength.

STUART   It wouldn't be fair on the others if you knew beforehand and they didn't.

GABBY   Others? What others? There's only five of us on the committee as it is, Joe was here a minute ago, that's you, that's Sally, this is me, and Gerry won't be here anyway. God, we were all here, Stuart. We could have had your damn meeting this evening.

STUART   I called it for Saturday.

GABBY   Tomorrow.

STUART   Yes.

GABBY   Different, is it, on a Saturday?

STUART   I arranged the meeting for tomorrow.

For those sixty-seven people there were twelve vacancies in the job centre. YTS and job share and part time and sweeping up in the local co-op. That's all there was.

GABBY   I give up.

STUART   A handful went to college. Putting off the evil hour.

GABBY   Are they all coming to the meeting? Is that what
           you're trying to say?

STUART   No. No. I just want you to think about them.

GABBY   Thank Christ for that, the hut's only ten by
           eight.

STUART   Someone has to show them that there's more
           than the dole queue. Competition, discipline,
           team spirit, excellence, training...

           Excellence! I wonder that you don't choke on
           the word. You devalue archery, reduce it to the
           level of 'Name That Tune'. Jostling the elbow
           of the archer next to you, so that you walk away
           with the big prize, the hi-fi, the weekend in
           Blackpool, the bale of BBC towels.

STUART   No.

GABBY   Excellence. Plastic cups sprayed silver, tin
           medals on safety pins. 'My name is
           Ozymandius, King of Kings...' And when the
           competitions are over and the medals are
           gathering dust on the mantlepiece, what then
           Ozymandius?

STUART   At least I'm offering them something. Time,
           trouble, training, a chance.

GABBY   Nothing.

STUART   This isn't some Eastern mountain. There's no
           cherry blossom, no yellow-robed monks here.
           We have to offer them something.

GABBY   Why archery? Why this?

STUART   Why? Because there's nothing else.

GABBY   Ah. The recession's version of 'because it was
           there.'

STUART   And because it's better than nothing.

GABBY   I once knew a child born with massive brain
           damage. Spent all her days banging her head

until it bled. They tried to stop her, with padded
helmets, hats, bandages...then they realised
that she had nothing else. It was all she had,
and it was better than nothing. Archery is not
just 'better than nothing'. The silver shaft
splitting asunder the golden womb. (STUART
turns away, exasperated.) Yes, something you'll
never understand. Never know. The raping of
the gold.

(GABBY *turns and stares at* STUART *then picks up the
bow and the bow stand.*)

STUART   Please. Give some thought to the youngsters.

(GABBY *walks off slowly.* SALLY, *her case closed,
follows him.* STUART *also packs up, talking as he does
so. As he talks* ZIP *and* JAMES *enter, taking turns
riding the bike.*)

STUART   When I started training it was 1966. I wanted to
travel. Lived in Milsham all my life and going
to college in Leicester. I wanted to travel, taste
the cosmopolitan life. I ended up in Lincolnshire.
Cosmopolitan Lincolnshire. And even there I
was homesick.

JAMES   (*shouting to* ZIP) Proper racing bikes can go at
seventy miles an hour.

STUART   But I grew used to the smell of cabbages rotting
in the fields, and I loved teaching those children.

ZIP   This un'd go at a hundred miles an hour if you
dropped it off a cliff.

JAMES   Ha ha!

STUART   (*shouting at them*) I thought you two had to go
home? (*Normally.*) I understood the children
then. I never made the mistake of thinking them
bumpkins, oiks. They'd grown up with each
other, knew each other, secure in a pecking
order that was bearable to all of them. Oh, cruel
still, I suppose, but not seeking to be cruel —

ZIP	(*to* JAMES) Your legs rub together all the way up.
	(JAMES *peers down at this own legs, pulls the thighs apart.*)
STUART	(*louder*) Not on the everlasting look out for opportunities for cruelty. There was...I don't know...
JAMES	It's only puppy fat.
ZIP	Oh. Is that all it is?
STUART	Acceptance.
STUART	And there were jobs. Jobs were swapped for the fun of it, jobs were.
ZIP	My old man got his giro today, I bet he got me summat.
JAMES	I wish my dad got a giro. I only get things at birthday and Christmas.
ZIP	He'll have got me summat. Come on, let's go and see.
JAMES	Wait for me.
ZIP	Come *on*.
	(*They exit.* STUART *watches them go.*)
STUART	It was the generation of the open end, that one. The open ended decade. An open door on the future. Like an old advert for cocoa or shoe polish. A poster of a threshold, and on that threshold a fat little foot on the end of a fat little leg. White cotton sock and shining black shoe. Start Rite. That was the name of a shoe. Optimism.

(*He shoots an arm into the air.*)

'Please Sir! Me Sir! Me, Sir! Sir! Sir! Sir!'

That was the days of Secondary Moderns and Grammers, and scholarships and grey school socks. We hoped for better. The eleven plus went and they brought in the comprehensives,

the CSE, and now the GCSE. From bad to
worse to bloody awful. Next year, what? Who
knows? I don't bloody know. I don't know how
anyone can vote for anything, believe in any of
them. A couple of years ago I had this really
bright lad. Leon Richards. Good at anything he
turned his mind to. I thought he'd be a chemist,
in research, or perhaps a physicist, and then I
realised that Betty Shaw thought he'd be a
writer, and that old razor Bill thought he'd be a
historian. God, he could've been anything. A
few years ago he'd have soared. Bloody well
soared. Then his dad was made redundant at
the chain works and his mother went on short
time, and he left school with a promise of a job
at the Carriage and Wagon in Derby. A year
later British Rail announced cut backs, and he
was one of them. I met him last week, painting
the outside of the Job Centre. Community
Service, he told me. He'd got drunk one day,
and smashed up a statue in the park, and now
he was painting the Job Centre and making a
good job of it. I could have cried, talking to
him. I wanted to hook my arm around his head
and hold him, like they do in all the American
films. I wanted to rock him, poor bloody
bugger. But Gabby doesn't care about lads like
him. For Gabby there's only Gabby and some
grand aesthetic target in the eastern sky. The
sun aflame over a bloody roundel, God in the
balance of his bow, and all of life's griefs and
angers split asunder on the yellow of a paper
target. 'Raping the Gold'! It's him that's been
raped, and me, and Milsham.

(*Collecting up his gear, he looks to where* ZIP *and*
JAMES *have exited, then notices the target.*)

(*shouting suddenly*) Don't worry about the bloody
target! Just leave me to put it away!

(*Realising the ridiculous spectacle he is making of
himself.*)

Shut up. Shut up, you fool.

(*His anger wins and he shouts again.*)

I'll just put every damn thing away, shall I?

(*Wincing at the sound of his own voice and covering his ears, he slowly gathers everything together and walks off.*)

Scene Two

SALLY *is walking home after the archery session.* LEON *appears in front of her, barring the way.*

LEON   (*singing softly*) Robin Hood, Robin Hood, riding through the glen...

(SALLY *stops and steps one way. He mirrors her. They look at each other.* LEON *slinks behind her, singing again.*)

LEON   Robin Hood, Robin Hood, with his band of men...

SALLY   (*her back to him*) I can't stop.

LEON   Who's asking you?

Got your bow and arrers then?

SALLY   My dad will be wondering where I've got to.

LEON   He just went up.

(SALLY *doesn't move.*)

SALLY   Well?

LEON   (*singing*) Loved by the good, feared by the bad, Robin Hood...Shit. I allus get that bit wrong.

(SALLY *starts to walk on again but he skips in front of her.*)

Talk to me then.

SALLY   What?

LEON   Say summat.

SALLY   What?

LEON	Well, not bloody 'What?'.
SALLY	Stop mucking about, Leon.
LEON	You're very 'Famous Five-ish', aren't you? Very decent and girl next door-ish.
SALLY	Am I?
LEON	Still, we live next to the local rent a cow, so it don't say a lot.
SALLY	Thanks. Thank you very much.
LEON	'Salright.

(*She steps aside and he mirrors.*)

SALLY	What do you want?
LEON	I like your voice. You always talk posh, don't you? Even right back in little school you talked posh. Stuck up.
SALLY	You know that's not true.
LEON	Like daddy.
SALLY	My dad's not stuck up.
LEON	Funny, innit? His name being Rawlings, mine being Richards. Funny, eh?
SALLY	Ever so funny. Now can I go?
LEON	Queue up together, we do, in the social. Your dad, my dad and me.
SALLY	I know. He said.
LEON	I bet he did. Bit of a comedown, eh? Bit of an embarrassment, is it? Lining up with one's workers.
SALLY	He didn't say that. He said it was a terrible shame to see a man like your dad having to line up for a hand out. That's all he said.
LEON	I bet.
SALLY	It's all he said. He saw you and he saw your dad and he felt sad. OK?

LEON	I saw these two little kids on the rec. They were on the swings and one of them fell off, and had this red black bloody knee, and he stood, crying. Then he went over to the other kid and belted him. Really belted him. Then they were both crying, see?
SALLY	(*softly*) Are you going to belt me, then, Leon?
LEON	I just want to talk. Your dad, I saw him, walking past in his smart clothes. Anyway, I thought...
SALLY	Tell me.
LEON	Every second Tuesday your dad and my dad and me go down the social and we walk through them double doors, and we're all the same. In the eyes of them girls behind the counter, we're all the same. Equality starts at the door of the dole room on the way in, see?
SALLY	Yes. I know.
LEON	Listen. Equality starts at the door of the dole room on the way in, yeah. But it stops at the door of dole room on the way out. See?
SALLY	I'm sorry, Leon...
LEON	'I'm sorry, Leon...' Bloody listen, then. See, when my dad got laid off he got two thousand quid. And he'd never had that much before, so he stuck it in the fucking bank and he's not touched it since. Frightened to, get it? How much did your dad get, then?
SALLY	I don't know. Quite a bit, I think.
LEON	I bet.
SALLY	But it's all gone now. The company car went so he bought another and there had been expenses with Mum, and we had to sell the big house...
LEON	And all my dad had were his work clothes, a jumper for Saturdays in the pub, one for

Sundays, and a 1960 radiogram. Don't bloody come the hard-done-to, Sally Rawlings.

SALLY   I'm not.

LEON   And your dad had the home computer, the nice stereo, the posh furniture, his flaming archery stuff, a house up the privates... Don't tell me you had to sell your bloody great mansion.

SALLY   I wasn't.

LEON   Have you ever lived in a concrete council house, have you? No. No, 'course you haven't. It's bloody cold, a concrete house is. No cavities, see? So you build up a damn great fire in the front room and the walls get warm and the cold air hits the outside and you get bloody great sweating patches. Damp. And the damp has a nice clear route from one wall through to the next, and it's all you can do to keep the black mould down. Bloody cold in the winter and fuckin' hot in the summer. On an average, it's ideal.

SALLY   What do you want us to do, swap?

LEON   So my dad signs on and your dad signs on and everything is equal, isn't it? And your daddy goes back to his central heating. We was getting central heating, then the council ran out of money. My old man gets up half an hour before everyone else to light the fire so my sister doesn't freeze in the mornings.

SALLY   Leon, it's not my fault.

LEON   And my mum don't have a nice fitted kitchen and a bloody microwave and a...

SALLY   (*shouts*) And my mum's dead.

            (*They are silent for a moment.*)

SALLY   (*walking away*) Let me past.

LEON   I forgot about your mam. I'm sorry.

(SALLY *stops and takes a step towards him.*)

SALLY   Why are you like this? We used to get on.

LEON   Yeah, till you stopped on.

SALLY   What difference does that make — to us?

LEON   It turns the clock back. My dad left school when
             he was fourteen because his dad needed another
             wage coming in. Your dad stopped on, because
             his didn't.

SALLY   My grandad was a labourer.

LEON   I don't know about that. I only know what I
             know, that my dad carted steel for thirty years
             and that your dad went away to college and
             came back a gaffer.

SALLY   That doesn't stop us being friends.

LEON   What'll you come back as?

SALLY   I haven't gone yet.

             (*She puts a hand on his arm, but Leon won't let
             himself be won over.*)

LEON   They'll never be equal, my dad and yours,
             because they was made unequal, different. And
             so was we. (*Pause.*) Mine looked at yours in that
             bloody queue and d'you know what he said? Do
             you? He said, 'It doesn't seem right, him
             queuing up here, with the rest of us.' Stupid old
             bastard. Stupid old bastard.

             (LEON *hits out at the air, fighting tears.* SALLY *grabs
             at his hands and holds them.*)

LEON   My dad spends all day reading the *Sun.* I dunno
             how he does it. It lasts him all bloody day. I'd
             understand if he was on page three all the time
             but he barely looks at that. I mean, for Christ's
             sake, what does he find to read in it? He sits
             there at the window with the bloody paper all
             day long. Sometimes he looks out, sometimes
             he'll move his head and look at the telly, but he
             sits there all day. What does your dad do?

SALLY	He used to get the *Guardian* and look for jobs. Now it's mostly gardening and archery. But mostly archery.
LEON	Mind, my old man has his moments of great, world-shattering activity. If the council workmen come to stick up a fence, or to put new windows in a neighbour's place, or to point a chimney or summat, then my dad's up and out of that house like a fuckin' greyhound from a trap. You seen those Road Runner cartoons? He burns sodding great trails down the road to the council offices. And if he hasn't got the same fucking fence, or the same window frame, there's bloody ructions. 'Fair do's' he calls it. Whether we want the sodding fence or not. 'Fair do's.' Stupid old bastard. Something for nothing, that's what he likes.
SALLY	But he's always been like that.
LEON	I know that, you stupid cow. He's never had any sodding money, so he's always been on the eye hole for something for nothing. That's all he's got — nothing. Least his way he gets something for what he's got. Ah...forget it.

(SALLY *walks slowly away. He's desperate for her to stay.*)

You could kill someone with one of them arrers.

(*She stops and listens but doesn't turn around immediately.*)

Straight through the rib cage, straight through the heart and phut! Out the other side.

SALLY	I suppose so.
LEON	You could get your own back.
SALLY	Is that a joke?

(LEON *shrugs.*)

LEON	It's all a fuckin' joke, innit?

(She turns away again but he lunges and grabs her.)

LEON   You're not going.

SALLY   Don't be stupid.

(He pulls her close.)

LEON   You're not going.

SALLY   You're hurting me, Leon.

LEON   Cry, then.

SALLY   You're hurting me.

LEON   You in't crying yet. Say it properly.

SALLY   Leon —

LEON   Say it properly, not in that posh voice. Say it proper, like in Milsham.

(SALLY slowly leans into him. His arms go around her.)

Say it.

SALLY   I don't know what you want.

LEON   *(squeezing her)* Say it.

SALLY   You're hurting!

LEON   Not like that!

SALLY   Leon! Stop it!

(He eases the pressure and she leans her head into his shoulder.)

SALLY   I don't know what to say.

(The light fades.)

Scene Three

GABBY is sitting at the head of a dining table. There are three empty chairs. On the plate in front of him is a wrapped packet of chips, from the chip shop. To his right another place is set with an identical plate and package.

GABBY *is hunched up and looks cold and ill. After a moment he suddenly gets up and goes, returning with two wine glasses. He places them by the two portions of chips and sits again. He is a dejected and smouldering figure.*

GABBY (*addressing imaginary guests*) Do start. Don't wait for me.

(*He glares at* SALLY'S *place and at the chip packet.*)

And thank you for being here today.

(*The phrase reminds him of other times. He leans back.*)

Thank you for being here today. I thought that we should come together one last time. One last time. Stop sweating, Derek, there are no sales figures to consider. And there is no production cost to excuse, David. And we have few personnel problems, Sylvia. A hidden advantage of the closed factory. The silver lining. It's an ill wind...as they say. And I have no brief. I have no brief.

(*He unwraps his chips and stares at them.*)

(*suddenly bright and breezy*) There is a meeting tomorrow. A committee meeting. Life is made up of meetings. Isn't it Derek? And Sally has just started. Out there in the dark, with a scruffy yob. Her first meeting. But tomorrow is 'special'. Secret. Ho ho! Heady stuff. Sod Stuart. Sod him. I have no fears of meetings. Eat your chips, Sally, and learn something. Derek here is a pastmaster at meetings. He went abroad on a final massive attempt to get some bloody orders. Didn't you, old chap? A final kamikazi attempt to get some work for our 350 men to do, to keep our heads above water, to keep the Nipponese wolf from our unsubsidised door. Old habits die hard, don't they, Derek? The expense account for that last trip was pretty steep, as was his habit...but then, he had been to Egypt the land of the greased palm...and we

understood. The credit cards, the rented cars,
the dinner and the wine...(*He raises a glass to*
DEREK.) Cheers, you bugger. Even the lads in
the foundry knew which day you were coming
back. It was like the whole place held its breath.
Oh, we didn't hope for much, we'd had your
telexes, and we didn't hold out much hope. But
the lads were hoping against hope. (*To* SALLY'S
place.) Sit up and listen. About that time Derek
and his latest live-in lover were building a new
house, a stone, neolithic cottage. Derek was a
go-getter, Derek was. Never made anything,
never actually produced anything, and he wasn't
actually any good at selling, but he was a bright
lad, our Derek, and good at meetings. Good at
dinners. The day he came back from that trip he
cut quite a heroic figure, with his jet lag, and his
brief case, and his weariness. As he walked into
reception, past the potted plant and the typists,
one of the foundry blokes was coming out of the
general office, and he grabbed Derek. 'Mr Ford,
Mr Ford, did you get anything?' and 300 odd
mortgages, 350 lives depended on that answer.
What did you say, Derek, do you remember?
You said...'Well, I got an antique door handle
in Holland and some very nice escutcheons in
Cairo.' Very good at meetings, our Derek. Just
a fucking prat at life.

Meetings are easy, once you have the knack.
The art within the art. Acting so well that no
one knows you're acting. That I'm acting.

(*He sits down again and chews on a cold chip.*)

Stuff Stuart and his poxy meetings. Those who
can, do, and those who can't...Listen, I know
my bank manager, I call my doctor by his first
name, and I am expecting an approach from a
head hunter. I can eat meetings.

Not even Access. Not even Barclaycard. No
figures to ponder. Nothing to add up. Nothing to

consider. Fifty five pounds a week. Eve dead,
the company finished, and thirty years to go.

(*He eats another chip and lifts a glass to his lips, then
realises it is empty.*)

I will have a little more, if I may. Thank you.
John Lennon has taken up with a Japanese
woman who wears no lipstick. He's brilliant, of
course, but it's a flawed sort of brilliance, don't
you think? (*His brittle laughter dissolves and he
slumps wearily.*)

They are going to take the gold. Oh, Christ.

(*He leans over the table, disregarding the chips. A glass
is shunted away, the tableware is dislodged.* SALLY
*walks in, goes to her place at the table and stares down
at the chips.* GABBY *looks up.*)

GABBY   They'll be cold.

SALLY   I'm not hungry now.

GABBY   (*bitterly*) Not for food, anyway.

SALLY   Not for chips.

GABBY   No.

(SALLY, *unmoved by her father, straightens the chips on
her plate and reaches over to collect* GABBY's *plate. He
holds her wrist.*)

GABBY   I haven't finished.

SALLY   They're stone cold.

GABBY   How I like them.

SALLY   Wine glasses?

GABBY   We still enjoy wine.

SALLY   Have we got any?

            (*Pause.*)

GABBY   No.

SALLY   I'll make some coffee.

GABBY   In a minute. Who was that?

SALLY	Leon Richards. He used to be in the fifth year, when I was in the fourth.
GABBY	You must have a lot to talk about.
SALLY	Not really.
GABBY	I see him at the DHSS.
SALLY	You know who it was, then.
GABBY	I knew he's Joseph Richard's son. I didn't know his name. He hasn't got a job.
SALLY	No.
GABBY	No lads at school then?
SALLY	There are lads. Yes.
GABBY	But you prefer 'Leon'. Skulking up an alleyway with a...yob like that.
SALLY	You like his father.
GABBY	It's not his father we were talking about.
SALLY	I think *he's* married.
GABBY	(*snatching her arm again*) Don't get clever with me, Miss. What would your mother have said?
	(SALLY *is sick of that question.*)
GABBY	I said, 'What would your mother have said?'
SALLY	Dad!
GABBY	She wanted better than that for you.
SALLY	People keep grabbing hold of me.
	(GABBY *drops her arm.*)
GABBY	You look like your mother. You don't have to end up in alleyways with the like of him.
SALLY	He's nice.
GABBY	Dole queue fodder.
SALLY	Your dole queue. And I don't look like Mummy.

GABBY   To me you do. More than Milsham muck.

SALLY   You sound just like her. Anyone from the
           Hollow, anyone serving in the shops, any of the
           friends I wanted to bring home, they were all
           Milsham muck to her, weren't they?

GABBY   She had standards. She'd rather have died than
           see you with him.

SALLY   Yes, well, she did. At least she wasn't a racist.
           At least she despised everyone...equally.

GABBY   She wanted better for you.

SALLY   She wanted nothing for *me*.

GABBY   If she had lived —

SALLY   You'd have been out on your ear. She would no
           more have lived on the dole than fly to the
           moon. One of her favourite little sayings. 'They
           could find work if they wanted it.' You wouldn't
           have lasted five minutes...'if she had lived.'

GABBY   You don't know what you're talking about. She
           knew I was unemployed.

SALLY   I know. She was too ill to damn well care...and
           they were the early days when everyone thought
           that there'd be other jobs, second careers, all
           that. But if she'd been well...if she was alive
           now... God, Dad, stop kidding yourself. Wine
           glasses and cold chips. Stop kidding yourself.

GABBY   You were only a child, you didn't understand.

           (SALLY *cruelly parodies a thin, bitter woman, nervous,
           chain smoking and ungracious.*)

SALLY   'My God, Gabriel, what are you feeding this
           child? What is this?'

           (*She fastidiously opens some wrapping on the chips.*)

           'Christ almighty! Bloody chips! My God, what
           do you think you're playing at! Sally — throw
           them away. I said, throw them away, child. Are

you telling me that you went into a fish and chip
shop and asked for these things? God, have you
no sense at all?' (*As* GABBY *listens he recognises his
wife.*) 'Where did you get that old jumper from?
I can't leave you alone for five minutes, can I?
And the child looks like a council house brat. I
thought we agreed that she should be a boarder
at senior school? What on earth possessed you to
send her to that bloody comprehensive? Oh,
God, don't try to explain. You really are a fool,
Gabriel. Well, we must put our thinking caps
on. There are people we know. They must have
vacancies.'

GABBY   (*answering her as if she was* EVE) I tried everyone.
             No one wants to —

             (*He stops, realising and horrified.*)

SALLY   Dad.

GABBY   People misunderstood her.

SALLY   They disliked her. It was mutual.

GABBY   She loved you.

SALLY   (*parody again*) 'Goodness, back from school
             already? Well, be a dear and pop upstairs and
             change, would you? Make yourself a decent little
             brat, there's a love. We have company, Uncle
             David, or Uncle Peter, or Uncle Tim, or Mr
             Porterhouse, or Mr Stretton.' (*As herself.*) There
             was often company Dad, especially if you were
             abroad.

GABBY   No!

             (SALLY *picks up the chips and throws them to the
             floor.*)

SALLY   Why won't you stop kidding yourself? I hate it
             when you talk about her. I hated her. I'm
             beginning to hate you.

GABBY   Sally!

SALLY	You used to be lovely! I remember running to you when you came home from work, sitting on your lap. You used to fool around, tell me jokes.
GABBY	There's nothing to joke about now.
SALLY	There is! There is! You used to read stories to me.
GABBY	You're grown up, Sally.
SALLY	I'm not! I'm not!
GABBY	Sally...
SALLY	I hate you and I hate your archery and I hate this whole damn town, and I'm getting out just as soon as I can. Leave you to your nothing.
	(*Silence.*)
GABBY	They were only friends, Sally. They meant nothing. I knew all about them.
SALLY	I don't hate you.
GABBY	I know.
SALLY	But you didn't know about all the men. Did you?
	(*There is a long pause. Slowly* SALLY *walks from the room.* GABBY *watches her leave.*)
GABBY	She was only a child.
	(*The stage goes dark.*)

INTERVAL

ACT TWO

Scene One

A corner of the archery field, the next afternoon. The lights come up on
ZIP, JAMES, LEON *and* SALLY. ZIP *and* JAMES *are holding bows.*
SALLY *is sitting down.* LEON *lounges, trying to roll a cigarette, but not*
succeeding.

ZIP   Knock Knock!

JAMES   Who's there?

ZIP   Annie.

JAMES   Annie who?

ZIP   Annie old Iron, Annie old Iron, any, any, any,
                    old Iron!

JAMES   Knock Knock!

ZIP   Who's there?

LEON   Shut up!

ZIP   Shut up who?

LEON   Daft bastard.

                    (JAMES *lifts a bow, like cupid and aims at* LEON.)

JAMES   Look, Zip. (*Singing.*) 'Little arrows in your
                    clothing, little arrows in your hair...'

                    (ZIP *joins in.*)

BOTH   'When you're in love you'll find those little
                    arrows everywhere.'

LEON   Christ. Haven't you two got some Lego or
                    summat to play with?

ZIP   We like watching. Don't we, James?

SALLY   Tweedledee and Tweedledum.

LEON   (*about his cigarette rolling*) I had an uncle could do
                    this with one hand.

ZIP   Went blind though.

LEON	I'll do you, wanker.
ZIP	Like your uncle then, eh?
LEON	(*giving up with his cigarette*) Shit. What we going to do then?
SALLY	I've got homework.
LEON	Don't be a prat, Sal.
SALLY	I've got to do it.
LEON	No one can make you.
SALLY	I want to do it.
JAMES	What is it, then?
SALLY	Biology.
JAMES and ZIP	(*leering*) Oooooooh!
SALLY	The structure of a wing, if you must know.
ZIP	Wow! (*Mimics.*) 'The structure of a wing...if you must know, James dear...'
LEON	Oy! dick 'ead! Shut your mouth, see? She wants to do her homework, arright?
	(ZIP *shrugs.*)
JAMES	All right.
LEON	(*to Sally*) Not yet, though, eh? You can stay a bit.
SALLY	I could. (*She looks at the boys meaningfully.*)
LEON	(*to ZIP*) Sod off. (*To* SALLY.) Still gonna get a good job and leave us, then?
SALLY	Who knows? But I'm going away to college or something. I have to get away, Leon. I have to.
LEON	Yeah.
	(JAMES and ZIP *begin to 'sight' the audience. Every now and then they pick on someone and shoot an imaginary arrow at them.*)

ZIP	That bloke there.
JAMES	Him?
ZIP	Him.
SALLY	(*to* LEON) What do you want to be?
LEON	Long term.
SALLY	Long term?
LEON	When you're long term you only have to sign on once a month.
SALLY	No, I mean it.
	(*Silence.*)
JAMES	I want to be a millionaire.
ZIP	You are. Already.
JAMES	Dad says we're the real working class.
	(ZIP *hoots with laughter.*)
SALLY	Leon...
ZIP	You and the cars and the double garage and the bloody holidays in Jersey.
LEON	I want to bugger it up for everyone.
JAMES	I'd quite like to be a social worker.
ZIP	Christ. Everyone wants to bugger it up.
SALLY	You once wanted to be a chartered engineer.
LEON	I once wanted to be the Lone Ranger.
ZIP	Who?
SALLY	You shut up. Leon, that's what you wanted.
LEON	(*shouts*) Before I grew up.
ZIP	I want to be six foot tall, muscles like meat pies, with a BMW bike and a flat in London.
	(*They are all silent.*)
ZIP	If anyone's interested.

SALLY	(*to* LEON) You could go to college.
JAMES	(*sighting a woman*) She looks like she goes to college.
ZIP	Get her.
JAMES	I did.
	(ZIP *gives an exaggerated version of someone dying — gurgles, gasps, the lot.*)
LEON	The giro's...
SALLY	Oh, for heaven's sake.
LEON	(*angry*) The money'd go down.
SALLY	No. It would balance out.
LEON	How do you know?
SALLY	It stands to reason.
LEON	There'd be books, and bus fares.
SALLY	You'd get a grant.
LEON	I'm too old.
SALLY	Leon...
LEON	Shut it, Sally.
SALLY	Leon...
LEON	(*shouts*) I want to bugger it up for everyone.
	(ZIP *whirls around and sights* LEON.)
ZIP	And all you're doing is buggering it up for yourself.
	(*Silence.*)
JAMES	(*to* SALLY) My dad says that your dad interviewed him for a job once. Said he was OK.
ZIP	Did he get the job?
JAMES	He says, thank God he didn't. I'm fed up with this.

ZIP	So?
JAMES	I like it when they see you and they look all shocked.
LEON	What, kids bows and arrers?
SALLY	Don't let any of the seniors from the club see you.
ZIP	You're a senior.
SALLY	Yeah. Anyway, you shouldn't have those bows, they should be in the hut.
JAMES	Stuart's cutting the grass. We'll take them back in a bit.
SALLY	Stupid kids. You don't frighten anyone.
ZIP	I will, one day.
LEON	Oh, yeah? What you gonna do? Breathe on someone?
ZIP	Yeah. That's right. And I'll scare them shitless.
LEON	Go on, then.

(ZIP and LEON *confront each other.* GABBY *enters, his hands in his pockets. He sits down somewhere in* ZIP's *sight. He is thoughtful, preparing himself for the meeting.*)

SALLY	Oh, leave him, he's just a silly kid.
ZIP	But I will. Frighten someone. (*He sights* GABBY *in his bow.*)
JAMES	(*seeing* GABBY) Let's go, Zip.
ZIP	I mean it.
JAMES	(*uncomfortable*) Come on, let's go.
ZIP	Bloody kill them.

(*There is another short silence.* ZIP *releases his imaginary arrow at* GABBY. GABBY *jerks his head up and sees* ZIP *at that moment.*)

ZIP	(*defiantly*) One day.

(LEON *turns, and upon seeing* GABBY *quickly walks off.*)

SALLY	(*calling*) Leon!
LEON	I got things to do. You play with the kids.
SALLY	Walk up the hill with me.
LEON	Get stuffed.
SALLY	Leon!
LEON	(*shouting*) I want to bugger it up for everyone.

(LEON *jogs away.* SALLY *slowly walks out, past her father. He doesn't look at her, still staring at* ZIP, *who becomes ashamed and awkward.*)

ZIP	Just mucking about.
JAMES	Come on, Zip.
ZIP	No arrows. Look.

(*Still* GABBY *stares at him.* ZIP *walks away, followed by* JAMES. *As they leave* ZIP *turns to look at* GABBY.)

ZIP	What's he starin' at, then?

(*They go . * GABBY *is left, in peace, on his field. He slowly grins, closing his eyes and crossing his legs.*)

Scene Two

The hut, next to the archery field.

STUART *walks in, hot and sweating from cutting the grass. He is wiping his hands and face with a handkerchief, and cannot see Gabby sitting outside.* ZIP *clatters up and drops the two bows at* STUART'S *feet, then runs off.* STUART *looks after him, exasperated.*

STUART	Where have you had these?

(ZIP *has gone.* STUART *shrugs and puts them side by side on the floor.* JOE *comes onto the stage carrying a card table.*)

JOE	Hello, then, lad.

STUART	Hello, Joe. Look what those little sods have been playing with.
	(JOE *isn't concerned.* STUART *takes three folding canvas chairs from nearby and sets them round the table.*)
JOE	Bit small for a meeting, isn't it?
STUART	There's only three of us.
JOE	Couldn't get the room at the pub, then? (*He sits.*)
STUART	Short notice.
JOE	Ah.
	(STUART *takes a letter from his pocket and smooths it on the table.*)
	Hush, hush, is it?
STUART	No. No. Not really hush hush.
	(GABBY *gets up and walks towards the hut.*)
JOE	We'll go for a pint after, shall we?
STUART	Yes. (*He is listening for* GABBY's *arrival.*)
JOE	Ah well...
GABBY	(*joining them*) Well, then?
	(*They don't answer.*)
	Well, then?
JOE	There's an empty chair, lad.
	(GABBY *sees the letter and stares at it as he sits down.*)
STUART	Well, then...
JOE	What's it all about, lad?
	(STUART *takes the letter out of its envelope and slowly unfolds it.*)
GABBY	Christ.
STUART	Perhaps, if I read it to you?
GABBY	Who's it from?

STUART	The town council Recreation Committee.
GABBY	Christ. Sally should be here.
STUART	Sally?
GABBY	She's the junior's committee member.
STUART	She's not a junior any more.
GABBY	Nobody said she wasn't their representative any more. We're not a quorum.
STUART	I told you, Gerry couldn't come. I phoned him. I read the letter to him.
GABBY	We're not a quorum.
JOE	Give over, Gabby. This is Open Bowmen, it's not the bloody EEC. If Stuart told him what it's all about and he passed his opinion on, then that's fair enough. The lad's not a liar.
GABBY	Get on with it, then.
STUART	Well, the letter is from the town Recreation Committee.

(*The lights fade on the Meeting and rise on* LEON *who is walking home.* SALLY *catches up with him.*)

| SALLY | Leon...wait. |

(LEON *stops and watches her.*)

Why did you run off? Leon?

LEON	You'd got your wing to do.
SALLY	What's wrong?
LEON	You've always got something to do.
SALLY	It's better than being on the dole.
LEON	I like it.
SALLY	Liar.

(*They soften to each other.* SALLY *sits down, smoothing the ground next to her and patting it.*)

LEON	Get piles.
SALLY	Not in September. (*Looking out over Milsham.*) There's someone in the old foundry.
LEON	Yeah. Bill Bartold and Neil Garnett got this book on furniture, and they've set up as restorers. Milsham's economic miracle.
SALLY	The small businessman.
LEON	Yeah. Got the book from the library, borrowed some tools from someone and bob's your uncle. (*Chanting.*) Easy.
SALLY	They make the foundry look lived in.
LEON	They reckon it's quite a good book. Thank God they never got one on brain surgery.
SALLY	Sit down.
LEON	You do what I do. I don't do what you do.
SALLY	How stupid.
LEON	Only in your posh mouth. It's how it is in Milsham.
SALLY	You watch too many old films.
LEON	What do you know?
SALLY	You're not making any sense.
LEON	I come from Milsham. Why should I?
SALLY	I come from Milsham.
LEON	Like buggery.

(*He extends a hand to help her up, she happily takes it and when she's nearly on her feet he yanks her so that she is jerked into his arms. He grabs her in a tight embrace.*)

You still in't said it.

(*The lights go out on them and rise on the meeting. STUART is exasperated, he has pushed his chair away from the table. Both STUART and GABBY are angry.*)

STUART	All they want to do is use the field. All they want to do is use the sodding field.
GABBY	(*to* JOE) Isn't there a club rule about swearing at meetings? Isn't there?
STUART	For God's sake!
GABBY	If discipline is to mean anything at all, Stuart.
STUART	You talk to him, Joe.
GABBY	Yes. Come on, Joe. I mean, it was you who gave Open Bowmen this field. Perhaps you have something to say about your gift being hived off.
STUART	Not hived off!
GABBY	(*ignoring him*) With the cricket club charging around, parking their cars on some damn loose chip car park, putting their score boards up on it, painting white lines on it. Boundaries!
STUART	One white line!
GABBY	All the yobs and the slobs of the town coming down here, walking their dogs, sniffing glue...
STUART	Cricketers!
GABBY	It won't stop at cricketers. It won't bloody stop at cricketers, for God's sake! Put up nice big gates, and a nice big car park, and a nice big slab-sided club house, and they'll all be down here. Bloody Matlock on a Bank Holiday!
JOE	It makes no odds to me if they come and use the field. I shouldn't like to think that a day would ever come when there wasn't a target put out on a Saturday afternoon, but there's room for both. Them at the road end, us at the river.
	(GABBY *looks at him in incredulity.*)
JOE	There's room, Gabby.
STUART	Of course there is.
GABBY	You hold your tongue.

JOE   (*putting his hands over his eyes and speaking flatly*)
               Right. Let's see if we've got this right. The
               council are turning the cricketers off their field,
               to build this here health centre thing. They want
               us to rent the use of the field to the cricketers —

STUART   At mutually agreed times.

JOE   For an annual rent.

GABBY   (*contemptuous*) A hundred and eighty quid!

STUART   Just their suggestion.

JOE   Open to negotiation, then.

GABBY   And who'll do the negotiating? Him? Lying on
               his back and having his belly tickled?

JOE   Gabriel. . .

STUART   And then next year they'll build us a club
               house.

GABBY   Us?

STUART   In the bloody letter. 'Compensation to both
               clubs'.

GABBY   They don't compensate you unless you've lost
               something, you prat.

STUART   We'll be losing nothing. Sharing. That's all.

GABBY   Sharing?

JOE   Hold up. Let the dogs see the rabbit, Gabby,
               lad. What sort of club house, then?

               (STUART *turns the page of the letter and reads an
               attached page.*)

STUART   'Self contained accommodation for both clubs,
               and a shared social area in the centre of the
               block, with bar facilities, communal rooms, etc.'
               But we could see the plans first.

JOE   Ay. We'd want to do that.

GABBY   So, you're all for it.

JOE	Like I said, I have no objections.
STUART	And Gerry has no objections.
GABBY	And the others?
STUART	We'll have to call a general meeting.
GABBY	Another meeting, then.
JOE	I'm sorry, lad, I think they'll go for it.

(*The lights go out on the hut. The lights rise on* LEON *and* SALLY, *still in a tight embrace.*)

SALLY	Leon...
LEON	I want to hear you say it.
SALLY	I don't know what to say.
LEON	Christ. It's easy, Sal. What you say is easy. It's twenty pence in your hand and the ice cream man coming up the road.
SALLY	Leon...
LEON	Listen. Pretend. Just pretend a minute. You're a proper Milsham girl, living in a proper Milsham house, down The Hollow. Your dad's sitting at the window, watching the reflection of Playschool, and the kids buggering about on the green. Your mam's at the kitchen table counting out her purse, and your kid sister's going from one leg to the other waiting for money to run up to the Paki shop. Now say it.

(SALLY *peers up at him.*)

LEON	Christ. Don't you even know how to pretend.
SALLY	What's the point?
LEON	There's a point. Listen you *are* this girl, see? And your bedroom's a bit damp, and your bed's covered with all these daft soft toys your mum gets from the Christmas club, and you never like them but you're gonna bloody have them 'cos she's put a quid in that club every week and that's the only money there is, and that's all the club's got.

(SALLY *has heard this before and she walks away wearily.*)

And there's nowt to do and nowhere to go and your mam says you might as well leave school sooner as soon as later and there'll be a bit more giro coming in, and maybe you can do a few hours in the market and get a few bob, and your dad says you can either go on YTS or bugger off out of it, because he's not having a layabout in the house.

(*He's near to crying now.*)

And you're nineteen years old and you've fucked everything up, and all you've got is what you could've been, what you'll never be, and a raging bloody temper and all you can do with it is slam doors and kick the fucking walls.

(SALLY *goes to him, cuts off his words with a kiss. They embrace. He lowers her to the ground and lies on her.*)

And this is you and this is me, and we're round the back of your yard, and I've got you tight, and you can feel me, and you want me, and there's nothing else. It's easy, Say it.

SALLY   (*knowing what he's talking about now.*) No.

LEON   You've not fucking listened have you? It's all there is. (*They struggle together.*) You'll end up with it sooner or later.

SALLY   No.

LEON   Why not? We all look the same in the dark.

            (*He pushes into her.*)

SALLY   No. Not like this.

LEON   I'll get you a flower. A bottle of wine. I'll nick you a four poster bed. We'll put it up on the dump, and lie there watching the sunset.

SALLY   Don't be silly.

LEON	I'll not let you fuck off out of it, Sally. I'll not let you come back a gaffer, and I'll not spend the rest of my life carting steel for you.
SALLY	Come *with* me.
LEON	Where? Nowhere. You'll have to come back here.
SALLY	Then we'll come back. Gaffers.
LEON	I don't want to be a gaffer. I want to be different. I want to pull myself out of the shit, but I don't want to stand on anyone else to do it.
SALLY	You just want to pull me into the shit with you.
	(*She struggles free and they both scramble up.* LEON *pushes her violently and she stumbles, falling.*)
LEON	It'd not bloody stick on you, would it?
SALLY	My father was right about you.
LEON	You bitch!
SALLY	I didn't mean —
LEON	You bitch. All I wanted was…(*He hasn't got the words.*)
SALLY	Leon —
LEON	You bitch!
	(*He runs away from her, exiting into the darkness.*)
SALLY	(*calling*) Leon!
	(*The light fades on her and rises on the meeting.* GABBY *is standing like an animal at bay.* STUART *is returning the letter to its envelope.*)
GABBY	So that's it? You buggers.
STUART	There's no need to be like that.
GABBY	What would you know about need? You bloody smug, tweedy bastard, what would you know about need?

JOE   We'll still be here. Open Bowmen will carry on,
               lad.

GABBY   Oh, will it? And before you go into a corner to
               have a pee there's going to be committees to
               ask. There'll be committees for everything.
               We'll have one, and the cricketers will have one,
               and the ruddy council will have one. One for
               cutting the grass, one for painting the lines, one
               for fixtures, one for the summer and one for the
               sodding winter.

STUART   We'll remain autonomous.

GABBY   You great soft sod.

STUART   There's only one layer of me a teacher, Gabby.
               All the other layers go way back, way back to
               the start of the factory up there, the chain
               maker's. Only the top layer is smug and soft
               and tweedy. Don't be fooled, Gabby.

               (*They stare at each other in frank hatred.*)

GABBY   So. You think you've won.

STUART   It's not you I'm fighting.

JOE   It's all out of proportion. It's not worth two
               good men at each other's throats. It's not.

GABBY   Oh, but it is. A holy war.

STUART   Christ! there's nothing holy about it!

GABBY   It's a temple.

STUART   A field!

GABBY   Everything is beautiful. Every sense is alert.

               (STUART *groans.*)

               For me. For me. This field is a temple.
               Everything is beautiful, even the sounds of the
               coal lorries rattling across the bridge. Everything
               has its own place, its own meaning. Everything
               stands out in stark, startling detail. Every nerve
               in every inch of me tingles. The spit in my

mouth is sweet with anticipation, senses
overflowing. And the bow in my hands is as
beautiful as any woman, more beautiful than
any woman. A bow is...perfect. A bow
is...Christ!

(*The word takes on a poignancy when he hears it.*)

Christ. The bow is a woman and Christ
and...something to be approached in bare feet.
And the walk to the firing line is a step in the
ritual, a promise, a flirtation, a threat. It's an
act of faith, of trust, of submission. A delicious
delay. And then the sight of the gold, down the
length of my arm. Oh, God, I ache with the
sweetness of it all. (*To* STUART.) But you just
forget all that, you call your meeting and get
your poxy vote for a brick built clubhouse and a
future of cups and medals and league tables.
You pull down the temple and build your bloody
amusement arcade.

STUART   It will encourage more members.

GABBY   I said, go ahead and do it.

STUART   We need more members.

GABBY   You do.

STUART   And they deserve to be members.

GABBY   Fool.

STUART   You can keep your temple, and we can build the
            club. We can have both.

GABBY   No. We can't have both.

            (GABBY *exits.* STUART *and* JOE *sit in silence as the
            lights fade.*)

Scene Three

*Inside the archery hut. Late in the evening, a week
later. The stage is in darkness.*

There is a tremendous noise offstage. LEON *enters*

wildly. He turns on a torch and waves it around erratically in the darkness. He is shaking an aerosol paint can, the bearing clanking inside it gradually taking on a rhythm.

LEON shoots an arm up Elvis style, and holds the torch as a microphone so that it nightmarishly lights up his face. He holds the pose for a moment but it doesn't develop into anything and he lowers his arm again. He sniggers at the trappings of the hut, breathless with anger. Resuming the shaking, he walks to one of the walls, taking the top off the can and giving an experimental squirt.

STUART'S
VOICE   You should do an outline first.

              (LEON *whirls around, startled.* STUART *walks out of the shadows.*)

STUART   Or at least know what you're going to do. You look as if you don't know what you want to say.

LEON   I know I want to say it.

              (STUART *sits down and watches.*)

LEON   You just going to sit there?

STUART   Why not?

LEON   Not going to stop me?

STUART   You're not my pupil now. You're younger than me, stronger than me. You've got a record. Why should I stop you?

LEON   It's your hut.

STUART   No.

LEON   Your lot.

STUART   As much yours as mine.

LEON   I'm not a member.

STUART   No. Not of the club.·

LEON   Oh, I get it. 'Think globally. Act locally.' That was one of them posters you put up. It's my club because I'm a human being, eh?

STUART   Something like that. (*Indicating the paint.*) What colour is it?

LEON	Blue.
STUART	I though it'd be red. Angry.
LEON	It was going cheap.
STUART	Don't let me stop you. What were you thinking of? Obscenity? Political statement? Profound philosophical catch phrase? 'Have a nice day.'?
LEON	(*peeved*) I've gone off the bloody idea now.
	(*They are quiet for a moment.*)
STUART	I'd like to do one.
LEON	What?
STUART	That. Graffiti.
LEON	Yeah.
STUART	Oh, yeah.
LEON	What?
	(STUART *gets up and holds his hand out for the paint, which* LEON *hands over.* STUART *shakes it once, thoughtfully, gazes at the wall and then writes in clear print: 'I care'. He pauses, then self-consciously adds a single squirt as a full stop.* LEON *looks at it for a moment.*)
LEON	Is that it?
	(STUART *nods.*)
LEON	Not much, is it?
STUART	It's everything.
	(LEON *looks at it again and then slowly walks around it.*)
LEON	Do you?
	(STUART *nods.*)
LEON	Why?
STUART	Once you've started you can't stop.
LEON	'I care'. What about?

STUART	Oh, come on, Leon.
LEON	No. Tell me.
STUART	I care about you. I care about this place. I care about all the other kids in Milsham. About my little girl.
LEON	It doesn't make you feel any better, though, does it? And it doesn't help me. I bet it won't even help your kid.
STUART	Perhaps not, but like I said, once you've started, you can't stop. It's like seeing something. You can pretend you haven't seen it, but you'll always know that you have.

(Pause.)

LEON	I keep thinking that I'm going to do something terrible.
STUART	Do you?
LEON	I don't know what. I smashed up that statue.
STUART	I know.
LEON	And I want to hurt people. Really hurt them. But I'm afraid to.
STUART	Hence the paint.
LEON	Christ. Pathetic, isn't it?
STUART	No.
LEON	My dad says what we need is another world war.
STUART	An old man's words. What do you say?
LEON	I don't know what to say. Not even an outline.
STUART	You're too young to give up.
LEON	I haven't given up.

(STUART pulls a chair up and gestures to it invitingly.)

STUART	What would you like to do with your life?

LEON	Don't be a prat.
STUART	What would you like to do with your life?
LEON	There isn't any choice, is there? That's like asking my mum, 'Which new house would you like?'
STUART	You told me you hadn't given up.
LEON	It's not a matter of what I want to do, it's a matter of what I can turn my hand to. Making the most of opportunities. Not grand ones, like you used to talk about, not careers and vocations and study plans and job satisfaction and all that.
STUART	What, then?
LEON	Shit. An old chair chucked on someone's bonfire. That's an opportunity. Over the fence quick and grab at it. Flog it off. See? And over at Oakwood, they landscaped all round the showhouses on that newest bit of the estate. Midnight, there I was, digging up the little trees, next day they were down the market, fifty pence each, five for two quid.
STUART	And how long do you intend to live like that?
LEON	(*stepping towards* STUART, *menacingly*) I don't 'intend' anything.
STUART	(*handing the paint back*) Fair enough.
LEON	I could burn this place down.
STUART	Yes.
LEON	I thought you cared.
STUART	Not about a hut.
LEON	We used to call you 'Andrex'...because you were soft and you went on for so long. And we could wipe our bums on you.
STUART	I know what you called me.

LEON   I thought you cared?

STUART   Don't pretend to be thick, Leon. You know
            what I care about. Not a hut, and not the names
            that kids gave me when they were still kids. I
            care about you.

LEON   Oh, piss off.

            (STUART *doesn't move.*)

LEON   Christ, if you was Andrex you'd be pink.

            (*Very slowly and with measured insolence* LEON *begins
            in one corner of the wall and sprays the paint right
            across the writing, obliterating it entirely. When it's
            done he steps back, and then, with a single burst of
            paint, he adds a full stop.*)

LEON   All right?

STUART   I think there's something you should
            understand, Leon.

LEON   Here we go.

STUART   I haven't got anything to say about your
            behaviour now. You broke a statute, fine. You
            only hurt yourself. It didn't worry me.

LEON   You failed.

STUART   No. Under all that paint, the words I wrote
            remain. No matter what you do, the way I care
            remains. I'll go home to my Missus and my kid,
            and I'll say 'Leon Richards? He used to be a
            really bright bloke. More brains to him that I
            could ever have. He used to be a really bright
            bloke'.

            (*Silence.*)

LEON   They want to castrate rapists. They should do
            summat to me as well. Take out my brain.
            Make me a happy moron. Everytime a kid looks
            like he'll be ambitious, or an engineer, or a
            scientist, they should operate on him. Or her.
            (*Pause.*) What do you want to do with your life?

STUART	I want to salvage something. I keep on trying.
LEON	Living in hope.
STUART	And perhaps one day this field will be more than just a field. There'll be a big posh clubhouse over there, and a cricket pitch there. And I measured out and there's room for rugby or football. . .
LEON	What about the archers?
STUART	Down there. A strip down there. Competitions and crowds of youngsters, fit bodies and lively minds, Milsham on the map.
LEON	Why?
STUART	Wouldn't you like that? To be part of that?
LEON	Fuck off. Instead of being an engineer? Talk bloody sense.
STUART	Think, Leon. Somewhere for the kids to go. You could join the clubs. There'd be something to do, something to aim for.
LEON	*(gazing at him in amazement)* You prat.
STUART	You'd prefer nicking trees and old cast-offs, would you?
LEON	You prat. I'd bloody well punch your stupid face in, but it's not worth the effort. You prat.
	(STUART shrugs and this suddenly drives LEON crazy. He dashes across the stage, grabbing STUART by the hair, yanking his head back, wrestling him on the ground.)
LEON	*(shouting)* Don't bloody offer me football and kid's games, or twenty five quid a week and a make believe bloody job. And don't you shrug your fucking shoulders at me! I could kill you for that. I could bloody kill you for that. Shrugging your sodding shoulders, like you was a world away and you could afford to shrug your sodding shoulders.

(LEON *gets up, kicks over the chairs, throws the table to
one side and knocks over the bin holding the arrows.*
STUART *has curled up into a ball.*)

You can't afford to shrug your sodding
shoulders. Three million people like me and you
shrug your shoulders. You can't afford to offer
me a bloody field and a football. Christ. Don't
you see that? We could kill for a job, people like
me. You can't afford to shrug your fucking
shoulders. I could burn this place down. I could
kill you. I could burn your house, kill your
child, rape your Missus, I've got nothing to
lose. (*Pause.*) And I masturbate in the dark.
Tears and semen. Nothing to lose.

(JOE *enters, putting the light on and causing* LEON *to
jump back in fright.*)

JOE	(*realising what is happening*) Bugger off home, boy. (*To* STUART.) Sort yourself out.
STUART	(*rising*) I'm all right.
LEON	Is that what you are?
JOE	Be quiet.
LEON	Old man.
JOE	That's right. (*To* STUART.) Are you fit?
STUART	I'm fine.
JOE	(*to* LEON) Big brave lad, aren't you? You pick your victims well.
STUART	I said, I'm fine.
LEON	(*wanting to go but trying to maintain dignity*) Bit late for you two to be out, isn't it?
JOE	Does your dad still strap you?
LEON	Ha!
JOE	Because, if he does, you'd best be off home, lad, before you do something your dad's going to hear of.

LEON	I'm nineteen.
JOE	And he's a chain maker. On his death bed he'll have more bloody spunk than you. Bugger off.
STUART	Don't Joe.
JOE	Oh, I know Leon. I knew his dad too, when his grandad arrived here, with his cardboard boxes and his Bush radio.
LEON	Uncle Tom looking for his cabin.
JOE	Bugger off, you daft sod.
LEON	I could do you.
JOE	Go on, then.
STUART	Don't, Joe. He's a good lad.
LEON	(*wildly*) I'm not!
STUART	He didn't hurt me.
LEON	I could!
JOE	A bloody two year old could hurt him. Now, bugger off, there's a good lad.
	(LEON *uncertainly backs away, into the darkness.*)
LEON	(*shouts*) Nothing!
	(JOE *picks up the chairs and starts to tidy up the shed, but then slumps onto a chair, tired and worn out. Long pause. The two men don't look at each other.*)
JOE	You were pleased with the general vote?
STUART	(*brushing himself off*) Oh, I think so.
JOE	You'll be glad to get it over and done with?
STUART	I'm glad it's over, yes. I just wish that Gabby hadn't taken it so hard.
JOE	It was unanimous, apart from him. That's what hurt. He feels alone.
STUART	Abandoned. Like his archery.

JOE	Ay.
STUART	He'll come round.
JOE	Will he? I don't think so.
STUART	It just seemed right. I mean, he was the only one against it.
JOE	Two weeks time! By, you wield a bloody axe and a half you do!
STUART	Do you think he'll come? To the do?
JOE	He's not a one for do's, our Gabby. Now, if Eve had been alive...she'd have given a bloody speech, that one.
STUART	I never really knew her.
JOE	No. She had bigger fish to fry. Or gut. Poor Gabriel. When you've known him like I have, since he was a boy, well, you can only have pity. She died of cancer, a year after the works closed down. They say that cancer can follow a shock.
STUART	When the mines started closing down heart attacks increased in mining communities.
JOE	And when it rains the road gets wet.
STUART	I mean....
JOE	Take no notice. That meeting left a dirty taste in my mouth.
STUART	Surely Gabby could have got another job?
JOE	In heavy engineering? No, he couldn't have got a job. You can only have pity.
	(GABBY *enters the hut, dishevelled and distressed.*)
GABBY	(*seeing the mess*) What are you doing? I said, what are you doing?
JOE	Just talking.
GABBY	About the bastard merger!

JOE	And other things.
	(*Pause.* GABBY *looks around, then remembers why he's come.*)
GABBY	I want what's mine.
STUART	(*not understanding*) What's yours?
	(GABBY *sees the bows on the floor and grabs one.*)
GABBY	This. I gave it to Sally. Her first bow. I lent it to the club. It's mine.
	(*He holds it to his chest as* JOE *and* STUART *stare at him.*)
GABBY	(*noticing the arrows*) The red flights are mine. I lent them.
STUART	They're all the juniors have, Gabby.
GABBY	They're mine.
JOE	Gabriel . . .
GABBY	James has parents. They'll buy some arrows.
	(GABBY *rummages through the bin taking most of the arrows. Sensing their stares, he stops for a moment.*)
GABBY	Stuart's good at replacing the old with the new. He'll get some nice new ones. Won't you? (*He feverishly resumes.*)
JOE	Won't you leave the bow? For Zip?
GABBY	(*indicating the remaining bow*) He can have that one.
STUART	Gabby.
GABBY	Shut your mouth. Pearls before the swine, these arrows. (*He looks at them and realises how battered they are, how ridiculous his words are.*) I'll take what's mine.

(*He turns and leaves, clutching the old arrows and the battered bow.* JOE *wearily covers his eyes.*)

STUART   Are you all right?

JOE   I'll be going home, now.

STUART   Are you all right?

JOE   I'm getting a bit bloody old for all this carrying on. Murderous bloody teenagers and good men at the end of their tether. Archery was a good pal to me. Not a lover and not a saviour. Just a bloody good pal. It was recreation. By, we're a nation trying to make summat out of nowt, and you can't re-create all damn day long. All this talk about teaching 'leisure skills'...it won't do. It won't do. Thas'll end up with men like Gabriel and men like Leon and sweating, smiling bloody monsters in between, like you. There has to be more than leisure. There has to be a village, a reason to get up, a reason to go on, a clock to clock in at, there has to be the feeling that you're needed. Needed. You have to know that if you're not there some bugger's going to wonder why, and wish you were, even if it's only to make his damn day easier. A lass or a lad has to be able to say 'What will I be?' and know that somewhere there is a chance for him to be something. And there's no one left in Milsham that can turn to a youngster and say 'I'll keep a place for you.' And that hurts someone like Gabby, and someone like you. It's a proper thing, saving a place for them that come after. A passing on of skills, a continuation of the pattern. But the skills are unwanted and the pattern's breaking up, and I want to be in my bed. You can only have pity. (*He gets up with great effort.*)

STUART   I'll walk with you.

JOE   Ay. I'll not let anyone harm thee.

(JOE *exits.* STUART *looks around the hut, and then follows, turning off the light.*)

Scene Four

*Late Saturday afternoon, two weeks later. A road, with
bus stops on both sides.*

The lights rise on ZIP *on a skateboard and* JAMES
wearing roller skates. SALLY *and* LEON *are standing
well away from each other, watching the boys' antics.*
JAMES *has a carrier bag which contains a pair of
old-fashioned beige slippers. He twirls it around like a
weapon.*

JAMES	Evil Knievel!
ZIP	Over 30 buses.
JAMES	A life saver in Malibu...
ZIP	Riding a wave...
JAMES	Grabbed by a shark!
ZIP	Knocked out by his own surf board...
JAMES	Leg off...
ZIP	Climbs back on...
JAMES	One legged...
ZIP	And wins the Malibu cup!
JAMES	Yay!
ZIP	What's in the bag?
JAMES	Nothing.
ZIP	Let's have a look.

(ZIP *skims over to* JAMES *who deftly avoids him. As
the two boys charge around the stage, shouting and
carrying on,* LEON *and* SALLY *studiously avoid each
other's eye.*)

SALLY	I can't stop long, James.
JAMES	(*surprised that she's talking to him*) What?
SALLY	I said I can't stop long.
JAMES	(*blankly*) Can't you? (*He stops.*)

(ZIP *dashes past* JAMES *and grabs the bag.*)

JAMES   Hey!

ZIP   Findies keepsies, Jamesie! (*Looking into the bag.*) Bleeding slippers! Pink bleeding slippers. Hey, Leon, James has got pink bleeding slippers.

JAMES   They're beige.

ZIP   Oooh! Beige!

JAMES   (*chasing* ZIP) Give them here.

LEON   Bloody kids.

SALLY   (*shouting to* JAMES) I'm going to Derby. Anyone coming?

LEON   Oy! Zip! Coming to Nottingham?

            (LEON *pointedly turns away from* SALLY. ZIP *and* JAMES *are in a tumble now, fighting good naturedly. They stop briefly and look at each other in amazement.*)

ZIP   You got the best offer.

JAMES   I've only got 10p.

ZIP   10p more than me.

JAMES   He must be after your body.

            (*They continue fighting.*)

LEON   (*over his shoulder to* SALLY) Derby's playing at home today.

SALLY   So?

            (LEON *shrugs.*)

LEON   Up to you.

            (ZIP *stops scuffling momentarily.*)

ZIP   They're playing away, dog brain.

LEON   Why don't you bugger off?

            (*The two boys flop back onto the side of the road, laughing.*)

JAMES	Hey, Leon, you coming to our open day tomorrow?
LEON	Bloody school?
JAMES	No. The field. The big do, you know.
LEON	I might.
ZIP	Everyone'll be there. Your mate Stuart.
JAMES	Did you really beat him up?
ZIP	Shut up.
SALLY	Everyone beats up on Stuart. (*She immediately wishes she hadn't spoken.*)
ZIP	Your bleeding dad took my bow.
SALLY	I know. He's not well.
ZIP	(*to* JAMES) He's gone...funny.
JAMES	Funny ha-ha?
SALLY	No. Mind your own business. He didn't want the cricketers to come.
ZIP	Yeah. If he had his way we'd still be fighting the flaming Sheriff of Nottingham. He wants to lighten up.
JAMES	That was on that video.
ZIP	So?
LEON	He really loves that bleeding field, doesn't he? I mean, like it was somewhere special.
SALLY	And to everyone else it's just a long summer evening and a bit of fun.
JAMES	Robin Hood and William Tell. (*He mimes shooting an arrow.*)
ZIP	A swift and silent killer.
SALLY	No, it's not.
ZIP	An arrow straight through the heart. Dead. (*He mimes shooting* JAMES *who falls to the ground, unconvincingly dead.*)

SALLY	Pack it in!
ZIP	(*picking up the carrier bag again*) What you got these for?
JAMES	I'm going to my grandma's later.
ZIP	So? She fussy?
JAMES	Oh, you know grans.
ZIP	I know mine. I have to put wellies on before I go in my nan's house. Cat shit.
JAMES	Really?
ZIP	Knee deep sometimes.
JAMES	How many cats has she got, then?
ZIP	None. She buys it in.
	(*They giggle.*)
SALLY	You two are all lavatory jokes and boobs, aren't you?
	(ZIP *postures, sticking his chest out.*)
JAMES	It's just the way his shirt hangs...oh, I don't know though.
SALLY	I'm going for my bus.
	(SALLY *crosses the road to stand opposite* LEON *looking to her side as if waiting for a bus. The boys continue carrying on.* ZIP *gets onto his skateboard, working it slowly.*)
ZIP	We done this big banner 'Bowmen welcome cricketers.'
	(JAMES *gets to his feet and skates again.*)
JAMES	Any my mum's done some cakes.
LEON	Cakes! Wow! And lemonade!
ZIP	The cricketers are doing a bar. Got a licence and everything.
LEON	I might come, then.

JAMES	Perhaps my dad will bring some booze.
ZIP	Isn't he sweet? I keep telling you, he's sweet.
JAMES	Stop it.
ZIP	I mean it. You'd not last five minutes in our street, James. We'd gobble you up.
JAMES	Get off!
ZIP	But we love you — all them lovely cakes in your mum's smart red and white kitchen.
LEON	God. Someone should tell her not to feed strays.
ZIP	She likes me. She said her kitchen was French Provincial. I thought that was a building society.
LEON	(*angrily*) Don't do that.
ZIP	What?
LEON	Make out they're rich and you're poor.
ZIP	They are rich. We are poor.
LEON	Every bugger's poor in Milsham.
ZIP	Gerron. They've got —
LEON	(*shouting*) Every bugger's poor in Milsham. (*The two boys stare at him.* LEON *makes his way across, opposite* SALLY. *He pointedly looks in the other direction for his bus.*)
ZIP	What a dick 'ead.
JAMES	Two of them.
ZIP	Yeah.
JAMES	Wonder why?
ZIP	Menopause. My mum's got one. Hers is early. She's got a menopause, a nerves and varicose veins. She's short of nothing she's got.
	(*ZIP and* JAMES *wander off and sit down some distance away.*)
LEON	Why you going to Derby?

SALLY	Why are you going to Nottingham?
LEON	Who says I am?
SALLY	Who says I am?
LEON	Yours doesn't come till half past.
SALLY	I couldn't remember.
LEON	Come with me.
SALLY	I'm meeting someone.
LEON	Ring them up.
SALLY	She'll have left already.
LEON	She won't mind.
SALLY	No.
LEON	There's nothing in Derby.
SALLY	Just as well you're not going there, then.
LEON	I could take you round Nottingham. Show you where things happen.
SALLY	Thanks, but I try to avoid fights and looting.
LEON	Oh. Thanks.
SALLY	I didn't mean it.

(*They are silent for a moment.*)

LEON	Your dad really ill?
SALLY	I think so.
LEON	Been to the Doctor?
SALLY	He doesn't think he's ill.
LEON	Oh. (*Pause.*) I'm sorry.
SALLY	Thanks.
LEON	Can I come over?
SALLY	I can't stop you.

(*He looks both ways and crosses the road to join her.*)

LEON	I wanted to say...
SALLY	What?
LEON	I'm sorry I knocked you down, that night.
SALLY	I slipped. You didn't knock me.
LEON	Only...I've been looking for you but you're always with your mates...and you've been staying in.
SALLY	My dad.
LEON	Is it because of me?
SALLY	(*shaking her head*) No. He's very upset about the club. It's all he's got.
LEON	He's got you.
SALLY	No. He knows he hasn't.
LEON	I know how he feels. The bus'll be here in a bit and you'll never hear what I'm saying.
SALLY	There's time.
LEON	Are those sods listening?
SALLY	No.
LEON	We had to learn something once for old Bevis, and he said 'Not Hamlet's bloody soliloquy, for God's sake.' So I learned this bit from the Bible...
SALLY	Go on, then.
LEON	'One generation passeth away, and another generation cometh: but the earth abideth for ever. The sun also ariseth, and the sun goeth down, and hasteth to the place where he arose. The wind goeth toward the south, and turneth about into the north; it whirleth about continually, and the wind returneth again according to its circuits.' And then there's a bit about the sea and stuff, and then it goes on:

'The thing that hath been, it is that which shall
be; and that which is done is that which shall be
done: and there is no new thing under the sun.'

(*He looks at her to check that she's listening.*)

'That which is crooked cannot be made
straight: and that which is wanting cannot be
numbered.'

SALLY   Not very funny, is it?

LEON   'For in much wisdom is much grief: and he that
increaseth knowledge increaseth sorrow.'

SALLY   Is that it?

LEON   That's it.

(*They are silent for a moment.* JAMES *and* ZIP *exit.*)

SALLY   You're very deep.

LEON   Don't.

SALLY   What?

LEON   Don't say bloody rubbish like that. You sound
like my mam.

SALLY   I only meant —

LEON   We're all deep, Sal, every one of us. That's
what makes it all so fucking awful.

SALLY   Increased knowledge increases sorrow. Do you
believe that?

(*Silence.* LEON *looks around bleakly.*)

LEON   Yeah.

(*There is another moment's silence.*)

SALLY   You didn't beat up Stuart, did you?

LEON   No. He's such a prat.

SALLY   He's all right. Does his best.

LEON   We all do that. Yeah, he's all right.

SALLY	You could come tomorrow, then.
LEON	I could.
SALLY	You can have a go with a 'bow and arrer', perhaps you'll stop going on about them then.
LEON	I'll have a go. I'm not joining, though.
SALLY	No.
LEON	I'll have a go. That's all.

(She grabs his arm and they run back across the stage to his bus stop, looking for the bus as the lights fade.)

Scene Five

Later that evening, GABBY's house.

GABBY walks on with a white sheet held out in front of him.

He opens it out, thoughtfully, and places it on the floor like a rug. A spotlight gradually comes up on the sheet.

He walks off and returns with his bow, his arm guard, his chest guard, an arrow, and his finger tab.

Very slowly and with ritualistic intensity he places these items on the sheet, around three sides of it.

He steps back and kneels down.

| GABBY | One last time. |

(He sits in the middle of the sheet, closes his eyes and begins his mantra. As he hums we see SALLY and LEON, walking, hand in hand. They pause and kiss. LEON goes, and SALLY makes her way towards GABBY. She stops when she hears the mantra.)

| SALLY | Dad! *(The mantra stops.)* Dad! |

(GABBY doesn't get up. He is shouting to her through a closed door.)

| GABBY | You're back then? |

SALLY	Have you eaten?
GABBY	What?

(SALLY *makes her way to him. At the edge of the sheet she stops.*)

SALLY	Have you eaten?
GABBY	(*shaking his head*) I want nothing.
SALLY	This is a sheet. What have you got a sheet on the floor for?
GABBY	Leave it.
SALLY	What are you doing?
GABBY	Leave it.
SALLY	(*looking at the bow and arrow*) Dad, what are you doing?
GABBY	(*sharply*) Minding my own.
SALLY	Dad...(*She moves towards him.*)
GABBY	(*shouting*) Off the white!

(*She jumps back. He scrambles over and smooths out the sheet where she stepped on it.*)

GABBY	Just keep your feet off it, will you?
SALLY	Shall I make you a sandwich?
GABBY	I want nothing. (*Looking down at the sheet.*) White, pure nothing. The empty mind.

(*Pause.*)

SALLY	Can I go tomorrow?
GABBY	Can I stop you?
SALLY	No. (*Pause.*) I'm taking Leon.

(GABBY *closes his eyes.*)

Leon said he'll have a go with a bow. (*He winces.*) They're doing a trial shoot for anyone that wants a go. (GABBY *starts his mantra again.*)

Dad! (*The mantra increases in volume as* SALLY *shouts against it.*)

SALLY There's going to be stacks of people there, Dad. A bar, and ice cream vans, and the cricketers are challenging us to a friendly. Stuart is the captain. Dad! Dad! Dad!

(*The mantra stops. His eyes are suddenly open, he points his finger at her, and very slowly and clearly he speaks.*)

GABBY You could have flown with the arrow. You could have soared. You could have soared.

(SALLY *slowly backs away from him. She sits down, gazing into space.*)

Scene Six

The archery field, the next day. The heartbeat from the opening scene starts, as the lights gradually rise until the stage is bathed in light.

GABBY *gets up from the sheet and very deliberately puts on his chest guard, arm guard and shooting tab. He stands with his bow and arrow at the ready.*

LEON *walks on and sits next to* SALLY, *his arm around her and their heads together as they talk and smile.*

STUART *and* JOE *walk on.* STUART *begins to struggle with a trestle table but waves away* JOE's *offer of help.*

ZIP *and* JAMES *run hollering and screaming, carrying a huge banner with the words* 'BOWMEN WELCOME CRICKETERS'. *They put the poles of the banner in fittings.*

Almost imperceptibly the heartbeat increases in both rate and volume. GABBY *slowly raises the bow and arrow. Everyone is moving around, putting out cups and medals, a tray of glasses and wine, and the boys break into another fight.* STUART *is at the centre of the stage.*

> GABBY *pulls back the bow, taking* STUART *as his*
> *target. The bow 'follows'* STUART *as he walks around*
> *the stage. Initially* STUART *is unaware of this while his*
> *attention is caught up with the others, but after a few*
> *moments he alone realises that he is* GABBY'S *target. He*
> *stands petrified*
> *at first, but eventually takes one step forward towards*
> GABBY *as if to stop him.*

GABBY   Stop there!

               (*The heartbeat stops dead.*)

STUART   Gabby — please.

               (*Silence.*)

GABBY   My arm is getting tired.

               (*His arm is shaking.* JOE *sees what is happening and*
               turns to watch.)

STUART   Gabby, please. Put down the bow.

               (ZIP *and* JAMES *are now watching.*)

GABBY   (*shouting*) What are you looking at? Look away!
               Look away!

               (SALLY *and* LEON *turn and see* GABBY.)

SALLY   (*shouting*) Dad!

               (LEON *grabs her. The heartbeat returns faster and*
               louder than before. GABBY *lowers his bow as if the*
               strain is too much for him. He raises it again and
               sights STUART *once more, then crumples to his knees.*
               There is a sudden burst of the heartbeat as GABBY
               clutches his chest and falls forward, dying.)

LEON   'What is twisted cannot be straightened,
               What is lacking cannot be counted.
               For with much wisdom comes much sorrow,
               The more knowledge, the more grief.'

               Blackout.

PROPS LIST

Archery Equipment

GABBY
A composite bow with an indoor shooting device attached, a set
of good arrows, quiver, chest guard, arm guard, finger tab and
a bow stand.

STUART
A composite bow, an archery case containing a set of arrows,
quiver and an arm guard and shooting tab. A bow stand.

SALLY
A composite bow, an archery case containing a set of arrows.

ZIP and JAMES
A fibre glass bow each.

ACT I

Clipboard and Scoresheets (Stuart)
Thermos (Stuart)
Boiled Sweets (Gabby)
Pipe and Matches (Joe)
Bicycle (Zip)

Dining Table
4 Dining Chairs
2 Plates
2 Knives and Forks
2 Wine Glasses
2 Packets of Chips

ACT II

Handbag (Sally)
Tobacco and Rolling Paper (Leon)

Card Table
3 Folding Chairs
Bin Containing Practice Arrows
Letter in Envelope (Stuart)
Handkerchief (Stuart)

Can of Blue Spray Paint (Leon)
Torch (Leon)

2 Bus Stop Signs
Skateboard (Zip)
Roller Skates (James)
Carrier Bag containing Beige Slippers (James)

White Sheet (Gabby)

'Bowmen Welcome Cricketers' Banner
Tray of Glasses
Bottles of Wine